LECKHAMPTON COURT

Manor House to Hospice

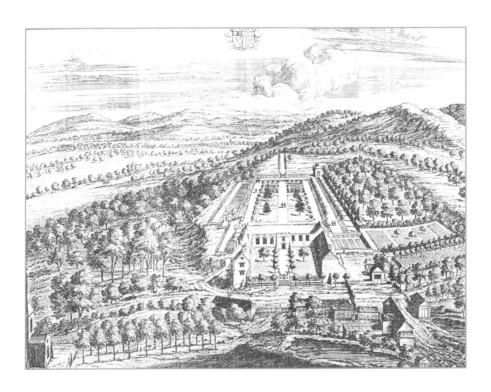

Engraving of the Court by Johannes Kip, taken from Sir Robert Atkins's Ancient and Present State of Gloucestershire, *published in 1712. Though some artist's licence has been applied, the general layout of the house and grounds is still identifiable today, including the avenue of trees leading down to the church, the lake in the foreground next to the stables and a coach house resembling a 'Tudor garage' to the right of the main building.*

LECKHAMPTON COURT
Manor House to Hospice

by Eric Miller

With a Message from HRH The Prince of Wales and a Preface by Mr Henry Elwes

For the Leckhampton Local History Society
Sold in aid of Sue Ryder Care, Leckhampton Court

Published by

Matador
12 Manor Walk, Coventry Road
Market Harborough
Leics LE16 9BP, UK
Tel: (+44) 1858 468828 / 469898
Fax: (+44) 1858 431649
Email: matador@troubador.co.uk
Web: www.troubador.co.uk/matador

ISBN 0 9524200 3 1

Cover: Leckhampton Court, from the West. *Adkins Photography, Witney.*
Title page: Leckhampton Court, main entrance. *Marion Norwood Callam*

The publisher makes no representation, express or implied, with regard to the accuracy of the information contained in this book and cannot accept any legal responsibility or liability for any errors or omissions that may be made.

Every effort has been made to trace the holders of copyright materials used in this publication. Should any omissions become apparent, the publishers will be happy to make the necessary arrangements at the first opportunity.

Typesetting: Troubador Publishing Ltd, Market Harborough, UK
Printed and bound by Cambrian, Aberystwyth, Wales

Matador is an imprint of Troubador Publishing Ltd

ST. JAMES'S PALACE

I have watched with admiration the development of the Sue Ryder Care Centre at Leckhampton Court since its opening in 1980, and I have been deeply impressed by the way it has responded to the many calls made upon it.

The local community has taken Leckhampton Court to its heart, and the army of volunteers and its fundraisers have created a home where medical expertise, practical compassion and a deep sense of peace exist in harmony. Leckhampton Court is a great asset to Gloucestershire and I am delighted to be its Patron.

As President of the Friends of Gloucestershire Archives I have witnessed a rapidly rising interest in local history and Eric Miller and the Leckhampton Local History Society have demonstrated this more than most. After the Church, researchers will invariably turn to the principal residence and the lordship of the manor for the next stage of study into any community and this book will be another valuable addition to the historic record of the village.

My own family's part in Leckhampton's history was small and my first recollections were of driving with my grandmother in the pony and trap from Colesbourne in the early 1940s. She loved to go to 'Leck,' as she called it, to collect loganberries in the summer. On the way home my sister and I had to walk behind the trap up Charlton Hill, pushing while my grandmother sat in state above us! Of course I have visited the Court on many occasions since and love the house and those who work so hard in it today.

Eric Miller's book now brings to life the comings and goings around the 'manor' over several centuries and it will be fascinating reading not only for those who have made their homes in Leckhampton but to a much wider readership too.

H.W.G. Elwes

H.M. Lord-Lieutenant and Custos Rotulorum

Contents

Message by H R H The Prince of Wales v

Preface by Mr Henry Elwes vi

Introduction and Acknowledgements 1

1 The Building 3

2 The Lords of the Manor and their Times 9

    I   Domesday, the Despensers and the Giffards 9

    II   The Norwood Family 12

    III   The Trye Family 16

    IV   John Hargreaves, Colonel and Mrs Cecil Elwes 19

    V   Life and the Community 21

    VI   The Leckhampton Foxhounds 26

3 The First World War: Red Cross Hospital 29

4 The Second World War: Soldiers and POWs 35

5 Leckhampton Court School 39

6 The Sue Ryder Care Centre 43

7 The Grounds Today 51

8 Personal Impressions of the Court 55

Bibliography 62

About Leckhampton Local History Society and the author 64

An engraving of Leckhampton Court, from Samuel Lysons's Collection of Gloucestershire Antiquities *published in 1793. The rather bleak rectangular building in the left-hand corner of the quadrangle, abutting the banqueting hall, was built after a fire in 1732 had destroyed part of the north wing. A space remained between it and the three-storey building to the left of the picture. The steps in front of the gates to the courtyard have since been repositioned below the main entrance.*

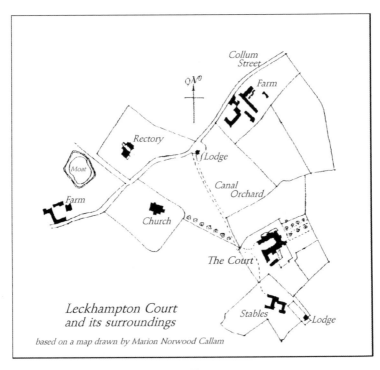

Collum
Street

Farm

N

Rectory

Lodge

Moat

Canal
Orchard

Farm

Church

The Court

**Leckhampton Court
and its surroundings**

Stables

Lodge

based on a map drawn by Marion Norwood Callam

Introduction and Acknowledgements

People are understandably curious about Leckhampton Court. Nicholas Kingsley, in *The Country Houses of Gloucestershire*, describes it as 'one of the grandest medieval houses in Gloucestershire', and it is certainly one of the oldest. From the Cotswold escarpment, and linked to the church by an ancient avenue of lime trees, it overlooks the road that passes through Leckhampton. As the principal manor house, it dominated village life for some six hundred years until the estate was broken up at the end of the nineteenth century.

Today, the Court will be most widely known for the Care Centre established there just over twenty years ago by the Sue Ryder Foundation, but it had other interesting and nationally important rôles before that. It was home to a Red Cross hospital during the First World War, the Second World War brought British and American servicemen to its grounds, followed by German prisoners of war, and for a time it housed a private school. Some aspects of the Court's history and its occupants have been described elsewhere, but those accounts are brief or fragmentary and some are out of print or not easily obtainable. This book recapitulates some of those details, together with archive material and information provided by private individuals. It is also complemented by photographs and other illustrations, many of which are rare or unique, since the Court has been well served by artists and engravers in the past.

A bibliography is provided at the end, and significant individual sources are acknowledged where appropriate. The Leckhampton Local History Society's first publication, *Leckhampton 1894 – the End of an Era*, edited by Bruce Stait, paved the way for this account, which also incorporates information to be found in the author's own *Leckhampton Yesteryear* and (together with John Randall and Amy Woolacott) *Leckhampton in the Second World War*. Marion Norwood

1

Callam's monumental three-volume *History of the Norwoods* has also proved an invaluable source. I also single out for thanks Rick Kedge, for his research on the sale of the estate in 1894, the prisoner of war camp and the school, and Terry Moore-Scott, for his research on the manorial estates.

Jo Blackburn, the Manager of the Sue Ryder Care Centre, describes its evolving rôle in the field of specialist palliative care. John Millington, Chairman of the Care Centre's Advisory Committee, has supplied a description of the work carried out by volunteers to maintain and improve the Court's surroundings.

The last chapter is made up of individual impressions, reflections and tributes from a wide range of people who have had a family or professional association with the Court. These offerings are no mere afterthoughts. At first I tentatively invited one or two people to write a few words appropriate to the occasion, but soon this part of the book seemed to take on a life of its own. The contributions which relate to the involvement of the Sue Ryder Foundation are especially moving.

I thank my wife, Margaret (who first had the idea of producing this book as a fundraising venture) for her patience while I was preparing the book, for her advice on content while it was still in draft, for selecting the illustrations and for her help in reading the various proofs.

Donations towards the project have been received from several sources, including two American citizens who are descended from the Norwoods of Leckhampton, Dr William Felton Norwood and the Reverend Matthew Corkern and his friends. The printing costs have been underwritten by the Leckhampton Local History Society. All proceeds will go towards the running costs of Sue Ryder Care at Leckhampton Court. The author appreciates the enthusiastic encouragement offered to this project by Caroline Williams, Fundraising Coordinator, and the Care Centre's administration.

Eric Miller
Leckhampton, June 2002

1 The Building

The Court has been enlarged and altered several times during its seven hundred years of existence. The following layman's account of the probable stages of development is based on an examination of the building's outward appearance, supported by documentary and earlier pictorial evidence.

The medieval hall

The first building erected on the site in the early fourteenth century will have been a simple 'hall house' (the central section of the house shown in the early engravings), a pattern that is still recognisable today. The front entrance, possibly sheltered by a porch, would probably have opened into a corridor, or 'screens passage', with the hall on the left and the kitchen and other domestic quarters on the right. A stairway led to the upper rooms.

Tudor enlargement

Towards the end of the fifteenth century, in the reign of Henry VII, new wings were built to the north and south, to form a U-shaped inner courtyard. The south wing, with its half-timbered upper storey, remains largely unchanged in external appearance. The domestic area of the hall block appears to have been enlarged and modernised towards the end of the following century. By way of confirmation, the date '1582' has been carved above a doorway leading on to the garden.

A three-storey cottage-like building at the end of the north wing, with a separate entrance on to the main courtyard, is also Tudor. It is the only part of that wing to have survived a fire in 1732 (compare the engraving by Kip). The cottage is built of stone with twisted brick chimneys and an oriel window facing down the hill. High on the wall

3

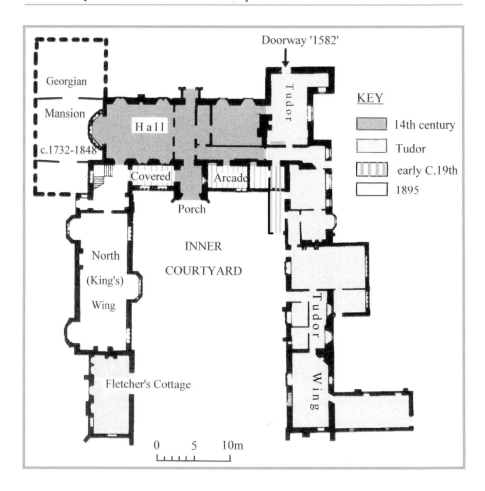

*Plan of Leckhampton Court showing the stages of development
(Based on plans published in the* Architects' *Journal)*

at the western end has been inserted a carved angel, of an earlier date, holding a shield ornamented with crossed swords and a snake wound round a dagger.

After the fire: the Georgian Mansion

After the fire in 1732 the cottage was left isolated from the rest of the building. A mansion in the Georgian style was added instead across the northern end of the hall. This explains the otherwise scarcely recognisable drawing of the Court shown above.

*Leckhampton Court from the north in the mid-nineteenth century, showing the Tudor cottage
isolated from the rest of the building after a fire and the Georgian mansion built on to the
end of the hall (from Norman's* History of Cheltenham)

Early Victorian Embellishments

In 1848 a corridor or covered arcade, with Gothic windows and battle-
ments to match the porch, was added to the courtyard side of the hall
block, and the curved steps were moved from outside the gates to a
position in front of the porch. The crumbling Georgian mansion was
demolished, which offered the opportunity of inserting a Gothic bay
window at the end of the hall, to a design by Francis Niblett of
Haresfield. Possibly at the same time or earlier, the hall and screen
were embellished with pilastered and panelled wainscoting, which
covered over the windows facing on to the garden.

Developments after 1894

A plan accompanying sale particulars for the Court in 1894 showed a
conspicuous gap remaining between the Tudor cottage and the main
building. The link between them was reinstated in the following year,
to a design by the Cheltenham architect H A Prothero. A library was

Francis Niblett's Gothic window at the north end of the banqueting hall
(Elwes family Archive)

created on the ground floor and a grand staircase was provided at the end which adjoined the hall. The Tudor cottage was stated in 1894 to have been used as a store, but during the First World War its ground floor served as a chapel for the Red Cross hospital.

Again in 1894, a passageway led to a full-sized billiard room in the rear courtyard. It was built of galvanised corrugated iron and was supplied with gas and heated by an open fire and a hot-water radiator.

The most recent renovation of the Court, by the Sue Ryder Foundation, is described in the final chapters of the book.

The Lodges

The three lodges – Tower Lodge on Leckhampton Hill, Middle Lodge and Lower Lodge on Church Road – date from the first half of the nineteenth century. Tower Lodge was based on an existing cottage. It had earlier been used by quarrymen as an ale house, when it was known as The Hamletts (after the landlord's name). During the nineteenth century the lodges were lived in by agricultural workers, including in one case a shepherd.

The Water Supply

The site lies on a spring line and was probably chosen to take advantage of a water supply. As recently as 1956, sale particulars have stressed the abundance of fresh spring water, collected in a large underground reservoir in the south-east corner of the kitchen garden. (The water was also fed by gravity to other premises, Church Farm, the Church Cottages and Ashmead Lodge.) To this day the lake is filled from a spring. Until the middle of the nineteenth century there was a long ornamental water feature or fish pond in the field (called Canal Orchard) below the Court, doubtless fed by water draining off the slope. The field between the drive and the churchyard is called Mill Hay, which suggests it may once have been the site of an ancient water-mill or wind-mill serving the Court.

The Court in 1826
From A New Historical Description of Cheltenham *by S Y Griffiths*

LORDS OF THE MANOR OF LECKHAMPTON

(date acceded to the manor, or first noted, unless otherwise stated)

1086	Brictric
early 1100s	Simon Despenser
1166	Thurstan Despenser I
1221	Thurstan Despenser II
c.1269–1295	Adam Despenser
1297	Joan Despenser, widow
1303	Amalric Despenser
1309–c.1316	John Lovel
c.1316–1322	John Giffard I
1327–1330	John Giffard II (first builder of the Court)
1340–1412	Other Giffards (including Joan, 1349–1354)
d. 1486	John Giffard III
1486–1509	John Norwood
1509–1512	Roger Norwood
1512–1561	Henry Knight, trustee, then Ralph Norwood
1561–1632	Trustees, then William Norwood
1632–1667	Francis Norwood
1667–1689	Henry Norwood
1689–1690	Richard Norwood
1690–1693	William Norwood
1693–1734	Revd Thomas Norwood
1734–1764	William Norwood
1764–1773	Charles Norwood
1773–1797	Henry Norwood
1797–1811	Charles Brandon Trye I
1811–1841	Samuel Lysons and Mary Trye, trustees, then Henry Norwood Trye I
1841–1884	Revd Charles Brandon Trye II
1884–1894	Henry Norwood Trye II
1894–1900	John Hargreaves (first private owner)
1900–1956	Mrs Cecil Elwes (Muriel Hargreaves)
1914–1919	Red Cross Hospital
1939–1948	Army camp, German POWs
1956–1976	Dr Paul Saunders; school 1957–1969
1977–	Sue Ryder Foundation

2 The Lords of the Manor and their Times

Although Leckhampton Court may not have the pedigree of some other English country houses, which have been owned by the same family since they were built, there has nevertheless been a remarkable continuity among its occupants. Over the six hundred years from the beginning of the fourteenth century to the end of the nineteenth, the Court was occupied by only three families, who were moreover inter-related by marriage: the Giffards, the Norwoods and the Tryes. They also contracted dynastic marriages with members of other wealthy and influential families. This chapter traces those occupants and relates some of their more notable achievements.

I DOMESDAY, THE DESPENSERS AND THE GIFFARDS

The earliest recorded mention of Leckhampton was in the eighth century, as the home farm of the royal manor of Cheltenham. By the time of the Domesday Survey in 1086, the settlement had grown in status and seems to have been divided among three landowners. One of these was a Saxon thane called Brictric and it is as the administrative centre of his estate – eventually to become the most powerful – that Leckhampton Court was later built.

Another house, clearly of some importance and dating from probably the fourteenth century, once stood on a moated site to the west of the church but had evidently fallen into disuse by the eighteenth century. Though it may have been the original manor house for the Leckhampton estate, it could equally well have served that function for a second holding of land, mentioned in the Domesday Book, called Broadwell (unrelated to the present-day house of that name, opposite Church Farm). Alternatively, it may have been related to another smaller landholding, which remained in being until it was bought up by others in the nineteenth century.

During the twelfth century the principal manor of Leckhampton belonged to a series of members of the powerful and feared Norman family of Despenser, who derived their name from the office of dispensator, or steward, to the king (and who were indirect ancestors of the Spensers of Althorp Park, Northamptonshire, including the late Diana, Princess of Wales). They also had the right as patrons to appoint a parish priest. Soon after 1316 the manor was acquired by John Giffard of Brimpsfield, a member of another rebellious family. A namesake was hanged at Gloucester for having allegedly plundered the royal baggage on Ermine Street.

It is not known whether the Despensers or John Giffard actually lived in Leckhampton, as they also owned property elsewhere. However, a second John Giffard, who had come into possession of the manor by 1327, left a lasting legacy. He is credited with building the nucleus of the Court as we know it today, the hall block, facing the entrance gates.

At the same time Sir John also enlarged the church, whose sanctuary, tower and slender spire still stand, largely unaltered. Inside the church itself are two recumbent stone effigies, which are generally accepted as representing Sir John and his wife. In addition, several heads which are carved in stone on both the inside and outside of the sanctuary could plausibly portray both male and female members of their family.

An imaginative description of what life may have been like at the Court under his remote ancestors was written in 1931 by Captain John Trye, the then Chairman of Cheltenham Civic Society. The Court would have been the only building for many a mile around that offered a large hall for public use, where the lord of the manor would hold his courts and meet his tenants. He, his family and guests and his vassals and retainers would all have their meals together. At night the family would retire to one or two very small rooms built on to the hall, and the rest would sleep in the hall on benches or on the floor on reeds and rushes.

Fourteenth-century carvings at Leckhampton Church. Those above are typical of several which probably portray members of the Giffard family, and the effigies below are believed to represent Sir John Giffard, who died about 1330, and his lady. The fact that Sir John's legs are crossed in the way commonly used to denote a Crusader is probably just a flattering compliment, as he lived after the last Crusades had been waged.

II   THE NORWOOD FAMILY

When another John Giffard died in 1486, the manor was inherited by his daughter Eleanor, who had married John Norwood, of Norwood (formerly Northwood) on the Isle of Sheppey in Kent. The family's ancestry has been traced back to King Harold, who died in 1066 at the battle of Hastings. No fewer than eleven Norwoods succeeded to the manor of Leckhampton during the next four hundred years. They lost no time in improving and enlarging the Court and established its U-shaped layout, and John Norwood probably originated the timber-framed south wing and cottage-like building at the end of the north wing, with its twisted chimneys and oriel window.

Roger Norwood, who died in 1512, was devout and generous to the parish church, leaving it money in his will as well as timber towards the erection of a new church house – a meeting place where 'church ales' might be held to raise funds. He was followed by his son Raffe (or Ralph), whose son Henry died before him. Henry was of some significance, however, through his marriage in about 1547 to Catherine Throckmorton, of the noted Roman Catholic family which still lives at Coughton Court in Warwickshire.

Their son William, who held the manor until his death in 1632 at the age of 84, was among the most distinguished of its occupants. He modernised the hall block and gave it new windows and chimneys. Through his marriage to Elizabeth Lygon of Madresfield Court in

The arms of Norwood and Lygon
Ermine a cross gules, NORWOOD,
impaling argent two lions passant gules
LYGON

Detail from a portrait of William Norwood by Cornelius Jansen
(Cheltenham Art Gallery and Museums)

Worcestershire he also for a time held a lease of the manor of
Cheltenham and played an active part in borough administration,
though still living at Leckhampton. In 1617, when a survey of the
manor of Cheltenham was carried out for King James I, William
Norwood was recorded as the holder of the manor of Leckhampton
and Broadwell, indicating that by then the two main estates originally
listed in Domesday had been amalgamated.

William Norwood was evidently not entirely conformist, for all his
status as a public figure. In 1577 he was listed as a recusant – ie he
refused to attend services of the established church. Given that his
mother was a Throckmorton, it would not be surprising if William
had Roman Catholic leanings.

After his wife died in 1598 William dedicated a memorial brass to
her memory. It was placed on the south wall of the church, in a corner
which has traditionally come to be used for memorials to the
Norwood and Trye families. The brass shows Elizabeth and himself,
kneeling on either side of a prayer stool, with their nine sons and two
daughters behind them. William's heir, Richard, died two years before
his father and it was therefore Richard's son, Francis, who succeeded
to the title.

Rubbing of the brass memorial to Elizabeth Norwood in St Peter's Church (detail)
(Amy Woolacott)

The Virginian Colonists

In the seventeenth century, especially during the political and religious turmoil of the Cromwellian period, many adventurous and enterprising young men went to America to seek their fortune. These included no fewer than five of William Norwood's grandsons and one great-grandson. That they were related to Sir William Berkeley, who was appointed Governor of Virginia in 1641, was certainly an encouragement to take this step. They all appear to have been staunch Royalists.

Today several thousand United States citizens are proud to trace their ancestry back to the emigrants William and Francis (while others are descended from John Norwood and Eleanor Giffard through the branch of the family whose seat is at Wykeham, Lincolnshire, and yet others directly through the Kent lines). A number of them have visited Leckhampton to discover their place of origin, and the author has met several of them.

The emigrant descendants of William Norwood included the following:

• *Richard*, who emigrated in 1643, and died in Massachusetts in the following year.

- *William*, who emigrated in 1648, married Lydia Jordan, and died in Surry (sic) County, Virginia, in 1703.
- Captain *Charles*, born in 1613, who was Clerk to the Virginia Assembly from 1654 to 1656. He returned to England and was buried at Leckhampton in 1692.
- *Francis*, born in 1636, who left England in the mid-1650s and died in 1709 at Gloucester, Massachusetts, where his house still stands.
- Captain *John*, who went to Maryland in 1645 and was later joined by his wife and three children. In Virginia he quarrelled with the authorities over the Book of Common Prayer and returned to Maryland, where Roman Catholic Royalists had greater freedom. He later became Sheriff of Anne Arundel County in that state.
- Colonel *Henry Norwood*, who was born in 1614, also set out for New England but after an adventurous life returned to occupy Leckhampton Court. He had fought on the Royalist side during the Civil War and in 1649, after the beheading of Charles I, decided to leave England. In his own account, *A Voyage to Virginia*, he described vividly the perilous sea crossing, during which the passengers ran so short of food that a well grown rat was sold for 16 shillings. Eventually the ship ran aground off North Carolina, where five of the party died of cold and starvation 'and the survivors turned their carcasses into food'. Henry Norwood and his companions were finally befriended by native Indians and, the ship having set sail without them, they were obliged to make for Jamestown by an exhausting overland route.

The exiled King Charles II appointed Henry Norwood Treasurer of Virginia (which entitled him to collect quit rents in absentia for the next twenty-two years) and he was at different times considered for the governorships of New York and Virginia. He returned to England to support the Royalist cause but was twice captured and spent two years imprisoned in the Tower before being exiled.

In 1662, after the Restoration of the monarchy, Henry Norwood was given the unhappy task of surrendering the English garrison at Dunkirk to the French. In 1664 he took part in an expedition that led to the capture of New Amsterdam (later renamed New York City) and brought back to the king the official news of its surrender. In 1667, having attained the rank of lieutenant-colonel, he was appointed Lieutenant-Governor of Tangier, during England's skirmishes with the Barbary pirates. Samuel Pepys made several references to him in his *Diary*, mostly friendly, though he referred disapprovingly of

Norwood's 'most proud, carping, insolent' behaviour towards the Mayor of Tangier.

While Henry was abroad, his cousin Francis was presiding over the manor. As Francis and his wife had nine sons and nine daughters (of whom all but two lived to be adults), he faced considerable financial difficulties. Consequently he was happy to sell the Court to Henry, a bachelor, who was easily able to purchase it out of income from Virginia. Henry returned to Gloucestershire in 1669 and soon immersed himself in local concerns, being elected Mayor of Gloucester in 1672 and one of its Members of Parliament in 1675. He gave a peal of five bells to Leckhampton Church in 1688, the year before his death. A bachelor, he died without issue and the manor passed in succession to the three surviving sons of Francis.

The third son was the Reverend Thomas Norwood, who inherited in 1693 and was instituted as Rector of Leckhampton in 1707. In 1732 a fire, caused by a neglected bowl of charcoal, destroyed most of the north wing. However, Thomas was able to replace it with a large three-storey Georgian house on the north terrace.

The last of the Norwoods to live at the Court was Henry, a grandson of the Reverend Thomas. The passing of the Leckhampton Enclosure Act in 1778 gave him the opportunity to consolidate the estate. During the following years he took out several mortgages, probably in that connection as well as towards the development of the Leckhampton Hill stone quarries. These had been worked since at least the early seventeenth century and were destined to play a large part in the fortunes of the Trye family who occupied the manor during the nineteenth century.

III   THE TRYE FAMILY

Henry Norwood died in 1797 without issue and left the estate by will to Charles Brandon Trye, grandson of Thomas Norwood's daughter Mary. She had married Thomas Trye, of Haresfield, south of Gloucester, whose family seat was at the nearby Hardwicke Court. Charles was the son of the Reverend John Trye, who had earlier established a family link with Leckhampton as its Rector from 1743 to 1766. The family claims Norman French origins.

Charles Brandon Trye, born in 1757, had already made a career for himself in the field of medicine and public health when he inherited the title to the manor. He was for twenty-seven years Senior Surgeon at the Gloucester Infirmary. He supported his friend Dr Edward Jenner in his pioneering work on smallpox vaccination and was co-founder of a charity for the relief of poor women in childbirth. In 1807 he was elected a Fellow of the Royal Society in recognition of his medical activities.

He chose to remain at Hardwicke, while the Court was rented out. For example, it was advertised to let in the *Gloucester Journal* in January 1804. He managed to discharge the considerable debts left by his late relative and was able to add some 200 acres to the estate, which he sought to improve through experimental cultivation. He saw the commercial potential of the quarries and had the vision and enterprise to construct a gravity-worked tramroad – the first known railway of its kind in Gloucestershire – to carry building stone towards Cheltenham, which was undergoing a rapid expansion as a spa town.

Charles Brandon Trye died of cholera, attended by Jenner, in 1811. There is an imposing mural carved in his memory in the north-west corner of Gloucester Cathedral, not far from a statue of Jenner, as well as a smaller tablet in Leckhampton Church.

At that time his heir Henry Norwood Trye was still a minor and the estate was run by his mother and her brother Samuel Lysons, the antiquarian. It is doubtful whether his mother remained at the Court, which was advertised to let in *The Times* in June 1814. Income from the quarries was supplemented by rents from land and property in Leckhampton and elsewhere. On the other hand, parcels of land had to be sold off piecemeal to repay debts and to cover the family's expenses, especially during Henry's undergraduate days at Oriel College, Oxford.

After coming down from Oxford, Henry played a conscientious part in local affairs. He became a Justice of the Peace and a member of the Cheltenham Board of Guardians, and served as Deputy Lieutenant and High Sheriff of Gloucestershire. He also became involved in a variety of business ventures, however, and invested heavily in the speculative development of the Bays Hill Estate in Cheltenham. When this went bankrupt in 1841, he was forced to offer his Leckhampton estate for sale.

The auction notice advertised tithe-free estates, a dairy and farm, three ornamental lodges and entrance gates and the quarries. The centre and south wing of the Court House were stated to be in 'excellent preservation', but the Georgian mansion would have to be rebuilt. Viewing was on application to Mr John Fletcher at the Court House. John Fletcher was the Parish Clerk, and from at least 1832 until his death thirty years later he was the tenant of the Tudor cottage, which was for long afterwards named after him.

The sale realised over £56,000. The Court and a portion of the estate were bought by Henry's brother, the Reverend Canon Charles Brandon Trye (the second). The Canon was soon able to pay off his mortgage and in 1848 set about reshaping the Court. Meanwhile, to escape embarrassment over his debts, Henry settled at Westmeath in Ireland, where he died in 1854.

During Canon Trye's forty-three years as Lord of the Manor and fifty-three as Rector of Leckhampton he was responsible for a number of significant local improvements. He had the first village school built in 1841. To cater for an increasing population he twice arranged for St Peter's Church to be enlarged (the vestry being erected at his own expense) and was the moving force behind the creation of a daughter church – St Philip's and St James's – for which the Trye family gave the site. In the family tradition, he served as a magistrate and was Chairman of the Cheltenham Board of Guardians, as well as Chairman of the Leckhampton Local Board, and was an early promoter of Cheltenham College.

The estate, however, did not prosper during Canon Trye's later years. With the Bishop's permission, he had lived in the Court from at least 1847, but in 1867, evidently for financial reasons, he moved to the Rectory house. Trustees managed the estate until 1880, with tenants occupying the Court. His son Henry Norwood Trye had been even more extravagant than his uncle of the same name. When an undergraduate at Pembroke College, Oxford, in 1853–1856 his expenses had amounted to £655 – nearly twice the annual profits from the quarries. More serious, the quarries themselves were running at a loss and no longer produced stone suitable for building. Henry spent much of his time at Hartshill, near Atherstone in Warwickshire, where he had a pottery firm, but in 1882 he decided to take over control of the quarries himself, employing as managers Neighbour Pearman (also the Parish Clerk) and his son Arthur. He invested in improving the facilities, and also erected a patent lime kiln, which was apparently a complete failure and never used. Output declined and in 1892 trustees were again called in to manage the estate. Before long it was decided that although the family would retain its seat and interests at Hartshill, further investment in the quarry workings would be unwise, and in 1894 the Leckhampton Court Estate was put up for auction.

One consequence of the collapse of the family's finances was that Henry's brother, the Reverend Reginald Edward Trye, who had followed his father as Rector of Leckhampton, also was adjudged bankrupt and was obliged to give up the living. He moved to Milford Haven, where he lived in straitened circumstances until his death in 1928.

Henry Norwood Trye died in 1902. The Trye family's connection with Leckhampton did not come to an end, however, for Canon Trye's daughters Mary and Eleanor (Meredith) continued to live in the parish (at The Grotto, in Moorend Road) and were staunch workers for the church. Henry's second son Captain John Henry had a distinguished career in the Royal Navy, which included a tour as Liaison Officer with the United States Navy Department in Washington during the First World War. He was a member of the Gloucester City Council in 1922, becoming an Alderman in 1931, and the following year he was elected Mayor of Cheltenham.

The Trye family's occupancy of the manor thus see-sawed between glory and disaster, but overall its influence and legacy have been wholly lasting and beneficial. It was in any case inevitable that sooner or later the estate would be split up and sold, and even if it was in one sense the end of an era it was also the beginning of an eventful new one.

IV   JOHN HARGREAVES, COLONEL AND MRS CECIL ELWES

In the summer of 1894 the local papers announced that Leckhampton Court, 'one of the finest old residential estates in Gloucestershire', was on the market. It comprised the manor house, its outbuildings, lodges, stables and land, plus Collum End Farm, while the remainder of the village and its surroundings were to be sold in 24 separate lots. The first auction sale was billed for 3 September 1894 at the London Mart, but it attracted little interest. At a second attempt, on 31 October at the Plough Inn, Cheltenham, bidding for the Court estate was brisk. The eventual purchaser was John Hargreaves, of Westhoughton, near Wigan, who was married to a daughter of the wealthy cotton miller James Platt of Oldham. (Despite his surname, and contrary to popular belief, he was not directly related to James Hargreaves, who three generations earlier had invented the 'spinning jenny'.)

John Hargreaves had in fact been the tenant from about 1872. During the previous two years the lessee was Captain W C J Burlton Bennett, who evidently sub-let the Court to him. When he became the owner, John Hargreaves was in a position to have the building extended. His new north wing will have been quite a contrast to the corrugated-iron billiard room that had earlier been erected in the rear courtyard.

Sadly, John Hargreaves's wife Edith died in 1882, when their two daughters, Evelyn Lucy and Edith Muriel, were still quite small. He died in 1900, leaving the estate to the second daughter, Muriel, who the following year married Captain (later Colonel) Cecil Elwes, the son of the noted plant-collector Henry John Elwes of Colesbourne Park. In 1912 fifty-seven acres of the estate were advertised for sale as building plots. Colonel and Mrs Elwes lived on in the Court until 1914, when the family moved first to Riseholme, Lincolnshire, and then in 1923 settled at Colesbourne. Colonel Elwes died in 1950. The family last stayed in the Court in 1926, though a few rooms were kept available for Mrs Elwes's occasional use. In 1955 Mrs Elwes died and the estate passed in trust for the benefit of her three daughters and today the agricultural land continues to be administered by the Elwes Trust. The last family event was held there in 1958 – a ball to mark the coming-of-age of one of Mrs Elwes's grandsons.

The Morning Room in John Hargreaves's day
(Elwes Family Archive)

V LIFE AND THE COMMUNITY UNDER JOHN HARGREAVES AND CECIL ELWES

Hospitality and Distinguished Visitors

It must have been like a breath of fresh air when John Hargreaves and his family arrived. He was well travelled and enjoyed a wide circle of friends and acquaintances, whom he entertained generously. In due course his daughters invited their young friends too, and the amateur dramatic performances arranged by Miss Muriel Hargreaves became a feature of the life not only of the Court but of the village as a whole. John Hargreaves opened the Court to the villagers for summer fêtes and this practice was continued for many years afterwards.

At a time when many of the inhabitants of Leckhampton were employed at the Court, the nature of the entertainments there, and the identities of some of the Hargreaves's guests, will have been common knowledge and the subject of local gossip. No guest lists or visitors' books are known to have survived. However, some notes left by an unnamed lady whose father had been butler to John Hargreaves may be regarded as a fairly reliable source. She recalled the splendid tables set for banquets and once having a peep at the ballroom when a military ball was taking place. She described 'gay times' when the Gloucestershire Yeomanry, of which Major Hargreaves had been a keen member, was training at Cheltenham before the Boer War. Distinguished visitors mentioned by her included three one-time commandants of the Yeomanry: Lord Fitzhardinge (under whom Lieutenant Hargreaves had served in the Berkeley Squadron), the Duke of Beaufort and the Marquis of Worcester. On one occasion, she claimed, the Marquis reviewed the Yeomanry in the field in front of the Court. Another frequent visitor was the Earl of Dunmore, an explorer, who instead of the usual tip to the butler would sometimes give him an autographed copy of one of his books (for example *My Journey across the Pamirs*).

An article in *The Cheltenham Looker-on* published in 1919, and therefore close enough to the events for memories to have been reasonably fresh, added the names of the Duke of Wellington and Earl Roberts among the guests. More importantly, the writer also stated that 'the late King Edward as a young man stayed in the house for the hunting to be found in the neighbourhood'. The butler's daughter too said that Edward, Prince of Wales visited several times in a private capacity. The Sue Ryder Care Centre has consequently given the name the 'King's Wing' to the north wing, which incorporated a suite over the library, reputedly for the future King's use.

It has also been suggested that the Prince brought Lillie Langtry to the Court. If he did, it must have been while John Hargreaves was merely the tenant and long before he had the new wing built, since the Prince first met Lillie in May 1877 and their affair was over by late 1880.

While their masters were enjoying themselves, tradesmen, grooms and cabbies went to the servants' hall and were given beer and something to eat. The butler's daughter recalled the stables and the harness room, where 'everything was polished to perfection'. There were two carriages, one of which was taken all the way to Carlsbad (now Karlovy Vary in the Czech Republic) when the family went there for the season, but it was left behind. The other is said to have remained unused for sixty years and was sold probably with the other effects in 1956. In possibly another version of this story, Alfred Miles, the Cheltenham carriage-builder, wrote that John Hargreaves had brought two buggies back from Canada, but he was unable to turn them on our roads and they were 'left to rot'.

John Hargreaves's hospitality was wide-ranging. In October 1895, after the new wing had been completed, he invited about 70 of the workmen, together with the architects and contractors, to supper in the new drawing room at which he complimented those present on the satisfactory way the works had been designed and executed. A report in the *Cheltenham Examiner* referred to the host's genial chairmanship, under which they all spent a very enjoyable evening.

Wedding Celebrations

The villagers had clearly taken Miss Muriel Hargreaves to their hearts and were excited about her marriage to Captain Cecil Elwes in July 1901. The parish priest, the Reverend Clifford Aston, performed the wedding ceremony at the Guards' Chapel, Wellington Barracks. He invited contributions beforehand towards 'a suitable present for one who has lived so long in Leckhampton, and, we hope, will spend many more happy years amongst us'.

These good wishes did not go unacknowledged. In the November, to celebrate their homecoming from honeymoon, the couple treated 300 of the older inhabitants of the village to a dinner in the School followed by dancing in the Parish Hall. Five years later, in celebration of their wedding anniversary and the birth of their two children, the couple offered hospitality to the whole parish. In the afternoon over 300 people sat down to a meal in a large marquee which filled the quadrangle at the entrance to the Court. Later nearly as many chil-

Cecil and Muriel Elwes with their first two children
(Elwes Family Archive)

dren sat down to tea, and then in the evening people flocked into the grounds to enjoy cricket and other games, while a band played. There was dancing on the lawn, and finally a grand display of fireworks. Clifford Aston thought that 'very much had been achieved by that one day of friendly comradeship amongst neighbours to strengthen the bonds of unity throughout all classes'.

Village Fêtes and Flower Shows

Since the 1890s the chief summer event in the village had been the Parish Garden Fête, which often spread out over several days. John Hargreaves was very willing to offer the Court and its grounds for such occasions, and the one held in 1898 must have been quite memorable, according to a report in the *Leckhampton Parish Magazine*. The whole of the ground floor of the Court was opened to the public and the quadrangle was turned into an oriental-style bazaar. On the terrace there was dancing round the maypole, and a ladies' bicycle gymkhana also took place. Boat rides were offered on the lake, using a vessel borrowed from the Liddington Lake Pleasure Gardens.

There was a ventriloquist act, conjuring and performances by Christy Minstrels and *Tableaux Vivants* ('living pictures' – a favourite form of entertainment of the period) in the old banqueting hall, while in the 'Court Theatre' Mr Prothero and his Company of Ladies gave a performance of *The Mousetrap* (not Agatha Christie's). The theatre was filled again with people anxious to see 'the far-famed mechanical and automatic waxworks' of Mr and Mrs Jarley.

A museum was set up in the billiard room, mainly devoted to curios collected by John Hargreaves during his foreign travel. A Chinese photograph, entitled *The Happy Despatch*, 'represented some high functionary in the pleasing occupation of pushing a sword with both hands under his fifth rib, and judging from his expression he is not enjoying himself'. It was explained that for a disgraced official this method of dying was the dignified alternative to execution. After John Hargreaves's death, the parish priest paid tribute to his 'generosity shown on that occasion, when for a whole week he surrendered the whole ground floor of the Court for various uses. We shall miss such a face, so long familiar in Leckhampton'.

From 1908 onwards an annual Flower Show was held in the grounds of the Court and in an adjacent field. It was a cross between a 'fair' and a 'show', but the main object was 'to encourage good gardening, good poultry keeping, and the keeping of good horses'. In 1921, as well as horse jumping, driving competitions, side shows and entertainments, there was a programme of athletic sports (governed by the Midland Counties AAA) and amateur boxing matches. A dance was held in the evening, at no extra charge. At the same time as the show about 2000 Public School Cadets were camped nearby, and their regimental band played in the Court grounds.

The pattern of village amusement continued largely unchanged, though by 1935 the Fête had been reduced to one mid-week afternoon. In that year Mrs Elwes was still the hostess. The day schools put on entertainments, and there were games – bowling for a ham, knocking the hat off, shooting with an air gun, smashing crockery – and a phrenologist was also on hand. Refreshments must have been lavish, since for ninepence you could have a good plain tea and for a little more you could eat as much as you wanted.

Concerts and theatrical performances

Before her marriage, Muriel Hargreaves had lent her musical and theatrical talents to entertainments laid on at the newly built Parish Hall. The most memorable of these was held in January 1899, with performances in both the afternoon and evening. 'Miss Hargreaves's Company' put on some *Tableaux Vivants*, when static representations of well-known paintings were accompanied by songs, readings or instrumental offerings. These included a mandolin solo by Miss Muriel and a violin solo by Mr G Hargreaves, who later accompanied 'Sleeping Beauty' with a song entitled 'The Jovial Monk'. Miss (Helen) de Lacy Lacy played one of the characters in a play written by her mother and stage-managed by her father. Other parts were played by Mr Julian Hargreaves and Mr C Elwes (already one of her close circle) and friends such as Miss V Hicks-Beach and the Misses Helen and Ann Forbes-Robertson. Meanwhile Mr John Hargreaves entertained a large party of friends to luncheon and dinner, winding up the day with a dance.

Colonel Elwes and the Local Community

A few examples for which records survive indicate that Colonel Elwes was interested in Leckhampton's affairs and generous in supporting its activities. It is therefore not surprising that he was elected to serve as Chairman of the Parish Meeting in 1912, and he remained in that office until he moved to Lincolnshire in 1914. He allowed local organisations to make use of his estate workers' club house in Church Road (now a private house named 'Old Farthings'). In 1906 the St Peter's branch of the Church of England Men's Society thanked him for letting them enjoy the use of those premises 'on very easy terms'. A rifle range behind the club house was used by a Men's Rifle Club and also, from 1909, by the newly formed Leckhampton Women's Rifle Club. Muriel Elwes's unmarried older sister Lucy was on the committee. The range remained in existence until the Second World War, when it was used by the Home Guard.

Although after 1894 the owner of the Court was no longer patron of the living at Leckhampton, there remained close links between the Court and the church. It used to be the custom during Rogationtide (normally in May) for the clergy and congregation of St Peter's to go in procession from the church up the avenue of lime trees to the terrace below the Court, where a service of Blessing of the Crops was held. It is not clear when this practice began, but it continued until the 1950s.

As a minor example of Colonel Elwes's concern for the church congregation, in 1907 he agreed to have the lamp lit at the entrance to his drive on dark Sunday evenings, for the benefit of those attending the service at St Peter's, while the incumbent had another lamp post erected nearer the church. Of greater importance, in 1913 he supplied some oak from the estate for a new pulpit, which was a memorial to the daughters of Canon Trye. Appropriately, this fine piece of work was designed by a Leckhampton man, the architect Leonard Barnard.

VI   THE LECKHAMPTON FOXHOUNDS

When the Leckhampton Court estate was advertised for auction in 1841, a selling point was the fact that a sportsman would be within easy reach of Lord Segrave's, the Duke of Beaufort's and Lord Ducie's Fox Hounds, 'with a crack pair of stag hounds upon alternate days'. The reference was probably to the Cheltenham Stag Hounds, which together with their quarry were supplied by Lord Segrave from the Berkeley estate. The stags were sometimes released on Birdlip Hill and might occasionally run through Leckhampton.

The Cheltenham Stag Hounds were disbanded in 1858 and the Cotswold Hunt was formed. Henry Elwes tells us that in 1908 his grandfather Cecil Elwes formed his own pack of foxhounds at Leckhampton Court. The hounds were assembled from various kennels, including the Cotswold Hunt. Some were loaned by Charles, Third Baron Fitzhardinge, of Berkeley. The hounds were housed in the yard behind the Court stables (now 'Goose Bay'), where loose-boxes and kennels were located until 1913, and they hunted the Painswick country and sometimes at Colesbourne Park. Once a season the hounds would meet at the Malvern Inn in Leckhampton Road. For the more distant meets, the horses and hounds travelled by train, presumably from Leckhampton station, and on one hunt a fox went to ground in the privy at Foston's Ash Inn.

Cecil Elwes's favourite hunter was The Continental, a good steeple-chaser and a terrific jumper. It had a sad ending in 1902, when it put a foot into a metal feed manger, severed an artery and had to be shot. Colonel Elwes erected a monument to him in a field behind the Court, where it may still be seen.

From 1912 until the start of the First World War Cecil Elwes was Master of the Burton Hunt in Lincolnshire. It is related that, much later, when in Alexandria, he came across a local Egyptian hunt and two of the hounds ran out of the pack and licked him; he recognised them as a pair from his old pack.

The Leckhampton hounds were evidently still kept on during the First World War, when the Court was used as a Red Cross hospital. In February 1919, the Cotswold Hounds met there before the Farewell Party.

It is not known whether there was a resident farrier or blacksmith at the Court, where in 1894 it was claimed that there was stabling for sixteen horses. However, it seems likely that there would have been. The coach house shown on the Kip engraving had a furnace and chimney in one corner, and could have served as a smithy.

A croquet match, with John Hargreaves and his daughters in the team on the left
(Elwes Family Archive)

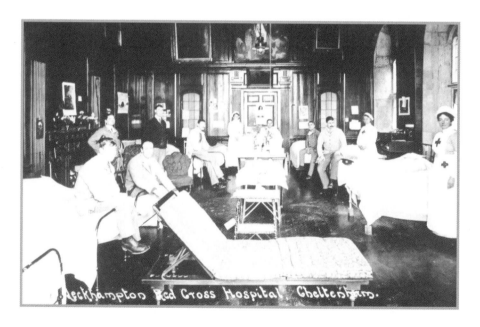

The Banqueting Hall in 1884, above. *A large painting of a huntsman hangs in front of the minstrel gallery. This was still in place when the hall was converted for use as a hospital ward during the First World War,* below.
(*Elwes Family Archive and Gloucester Record Office/David Bick*)

3 The First World War: Red Cross Hospital

During the First World War Colonel and Mrs Elwes placed the Court at the disposal of the British Red Cross to use as a hospital for sick and wounded soldiers. It opened in February 1915 and closed four years later. The staff were members of the Gloucestershire Voluntary Aid Detachment (VAD) No 42, which had been formed as early as 1910, anticipating that there would soon be a need for its services. Thus the local community rallied together in a way that is echoed today by the groups offering support to the Sue Ryder Care Centre. The illustrated souvenir booklet which was produced after the war provides much information on different aspects of life at the Court during that time. Some of it is summarised below, and this chapter offers an opportunity to honour again the men and especially the women who ran the hospital and to remind us of the bustling community to which the Court was home.

The booklet listed the names, ranks, regiments and dates of most of the 1700 British, Commonwealth and Belgian soldiers who had been cared for. The hospital opened with fifty beds, but these were increased to a hundred after the Somme offensive in July 1916.

The Commandant, Mrs Grace Ward, paid tribute in a foreword to the tenacity, courage and cheerfulness of 'our soldier boys' but believed there was just as much honour due to 'our girls, who have shown such patience, pluck, and energy, under trying conditions of new, unexpected and often uncongenial work. I have never seen a black look, nor heard a grumble, at any order given.'

Among the medical officers was Dr H Lloyd-Davies, the popular general practitioner after whom a local surgery has since been named.

Red Cross Hospital medical and senior nursing staff during the First World War.
Dr McAldowie is on extreme right of back row, next to Dr Lloyd-Davies. Mrs Ward is
front row centre, with Miss Whishaw on her left.

Over sixty nurses were mentioned, of whom eighteen served throughout the war. Fifty cooks and pantrymaids and over sixty male orderlies
were present for some or all of the time. Their names, along with
those of other volunteers, read like a roll-call of Leckhampton's
notable families. Local clergy acted as chaplains.

Large wards were laid out in the banqueting hall and the ground
floor of the north wing, with smaller ones in the bedrooms above,
terminating in the upstairs room in Fletcher's Cottage (above the
then chapel). The ground floor of the Tudor wing was used for
bedrooms for the staff, the quarter-master's room, the kitchen,
scullery and dining room. Above were the surgery and operating
theatre, and at the foot of the stairs was the passage which led to the
billiard and concert room. The Commandant's office looked on to the
croquet lawn, next to the nurses' sitting room 'with its low roof and
black wainscoting and delightful view on to the rose garden', where
the ladies' sewing party met on two afternoons a week under the lead-
ership of Mrs Leonard Barnard.

Dr McAldowie, the senior medical officer, recalled the arrival of
mud-caked, blood-stained warriors straight from the battlefields, the

first field dressings still round their limbs or heads. He gave graphic descriptions of some of the wounds the medical staff had to deal with and expressed satisfaction at the 'many happy, useful hours we spent in our bright little operation theatre'. They gradually acquired a knowledge of previously unfamiliar injuries and ailments: trench foot, gas gangrene from gunshot wounds, and gas poisoning, for all of which text-book knowledge proved useless. Others arrived from Salonika and East Africa, suffering from malaria, and one of the last convoys brought only cases of influenza.

The 'boys' played ghoulish jokes on each other before the operations and observed with amusement as patients came round from the intoxicating effects of the anaesthetic. There were many severe cases, however, both medical and surgical, but in spite of that there were only two deaths, neither of them from wounds sustained in battle.

Some remarkable recoveries were recorded, such as a musician who despite a shattered arm was able later to entertain with many brilliant performances on the piano, and an Australian with a compound fracture of the skull, thought to be a hopeless case, but who recovered completely and 'was able to resume bush life'. One patient had epilepsy following a brain injury; it was considered that the man's fits should not interfere with his work in civilian life, but this opinion was promptly altered when it was learnt that he was a steeple-jack by trade!

To entertain the men, the staff arranged concerts, dances, plays and whist-drives. Summer fêtes raised money for the 'luxury account', which was spent on things not provided by the War Office allowance. Bright summer days were recalled, 'with our boys in blue [hospital uniform] lying in scattered groups under the great trees, or on grassy terraces in the beautiful grounds'.

Sports played an important part in restoring the patients' health and keeping up their spirits, and teams competed against those from the eight other such hospitals in the area. Appropriately, shooting was regarded as an important pursuit, and practice took place on a miniature range set up at the Court. The Leckhampton team was seldom without a good billiards team, for which it regularly won the cup. Both billiards and snooker were popular, and handicaps among the patients were played off for prizes of cigarettes. Surprisingly, by comparison with the pursuits of today's young men, little interest was shown in football 'as so few people played the association game'. There was more enthusiasm for cricket and some enjoyable matches were also arranged between the patients and the sisters, the patients being allowed only to bowl underhand and bat left handed.

Several mementos of the hospital are held in the Gloucestershire Record Office. A 'Gift Book' lists meticulously all the donations of money and in kind, together with their values, made between April 1916 and March 1919. There were standard headings for cakes, eggs, vegetables, flour, fowl, cigarettes, pillow cases, jam and potatoes. Some examples are:

Donation	Miss Hargreaves	£2
84 eggs	Pilley Band of Hope	8s.6d
12 eggs	Miss Laurence, Whittington Court	1s.3d
2 doz Bengall Chutney	'Buckler'	1s.
1 box Woodbines	Mr Shipley	5s.6d
4500 cigarettes	Mr Shipley	£4.10s.0d
5 sacks greens	Mrs Barnard	9d
absorbent wool, bandages, 30 pr braces,9 pillows, h'chieves, etc	Mrs Thompson, New York	£3.0s.0d
12 prs sheets	Lady Mayoress	£7.0s.0d
11 prs sheets	} Queen Mary's Needlework Guild	£6.10s.0d
50 pillow cases		£2.10s.0d
6 pillows		£1.0s.0d

Of especial interest are two scrapbooks recently deposited by David Bick, containing drawings, photographs and correspondence. They had been kept by two of the young ladies on the staff: Edith Harland, the 'Colonial Visitor', and Gladys Duckworth, who had worked as a cook throughout the war. (Miss Harland's address was Rosenho(e), 30 Moorend Road. After the war local directories show *Mrs* Duckworth as the occupant.)

The books included numerous affectionate and humorous messages to their owners: 'a kind mother to all the boys', 'great kindness to wounded Tommies', 'many thanks for all the enjoyable outings during my stay', 'many thanks ... especially for the buck-shee lunches'. Some of those who wrote in Miss Duckworth's book were members of 'the Mysterious Order of Spud Peelers'.

It is clear that Miss Harland's car was as popular as Miss Harland herself. A friend, writing from the British Expeditionary Force in 1916, hoped that 'the little car is still going well'. A photograph showing patients and the front part of a car (a Standard), registration No AD 1925 and 'VOL ORG CLUB' on the windscreen, was surely hers. Her scrapbook contains a letter from the Duchess of Beaufort, Chairman of the Gloucestershire Association for Voluntary Organisations, thanking her for 'the splendid way in which you helped

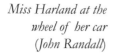

Miss Harland at the wheel of her car (John Randall)

by lending your car (and personally defraying the expenses of transport of same) to the County Depot for Voluntary Organisations'.

A photograph album, held in the Sue Ryder Care Centre, shows many of the soldiers, medical staff, orderlies and other helpers in a variety of poses, mostly in relaxed groups taking their ease in the grounds of the Court. One photograph shows them on board a heavily laden pleasure cruiser, the 'SS *King*' at Tewkesbury. Others show a crowd at Pershore, having been ferried in cars and char-a-bancs on Cheltenham Soldiers' Day ('Motor trip for soldiers from Red Cross Hospitals'). In others we see groups taking tea in the garden of a grand house at Worcester. The album was compiled by a Canadian patient, Private William Platt. (By chance, Platt was also the maiden name of John Hargreaves's wife).

Several of the staff received official recognition for their service. Mrs Grace Ward was invested at Buckingham Palace with the order of Member of the British Empire, Sister Lucy Hills, the 'Lady Superintendent', received a Red Cross honour, and Miss Evelyn Crane received the Belgian Médaille de la Reine Elizabeth, avec Croix Rouge. Others who had served throughout or otherwise distinguished themselves were mentioned in dispatches, including Miss Lilian Whishaw, the Quartermaster, Miss J Ormerod, the Assistant Commandant, Miss J Bourne, the Housekeeper and Head Cook, and Staff Nurse Mrs A Savile, and Mr P H H Kenworthy, Quartermaster to the male Orderlies. (Miss Whishaw was the half-sister of Frederick Whishaw, who in 1891 had lived at The Grotto in Moorend Road, later occupied by Canon Trye's daughters. She was related to the mother of Dr Edward Wilson, of The Crippetts, who died with Captain Scott in Antarctica.)

A party to celebrate the fourth anniversary of the hospital's opening was held on 27 February 1919, attended by 300 guests, many of them in fancy dress. The proceedings were presided over by Mr Sydney Harrison, Honorary Secretary of the hospital and editor of the souvenir booklet (and also Cheltenham Borough Librarian). Presentations, with warm speeches of praise, were offered to Mrs Ward and Miss Whishaw by Drs McAldowie and Lloyd-Davies. Mrs Ward received a silver salver and tea service, together with a vellum-bound list of subscribers and a pen-and-ink sketch of the Court by Miss N Hills, of the Cheltenham School of Art.

As the party was being held, there were still fifty patients at the Court, and these were joined two days later by others from the Racecourse hospital, which was closing down. On 2 April 1919 the last patients left the Court. The event was marked by a service of thanksgiving and a special celebration of Holy Eucharist for members of the staff at St Peter's Church, presided over by the Reverend J Austin Hodson, Rector of Leckhampton.

Soldiers setting off for a day out at Pershore
(Gloucestershire Record Office/David Bick)

4 The Second World War: Soldiers and POWs

British and American Troops

From 1939 to 1948 the Court, its grounds, the fields and orchards were requisitioned by the War Office. Nissen huts were erected in the fields and orchards below the Court. Some of the concrete bases may still be seen, but most were taken up when the houses in Collum End Rise were built. During those ten years the Court was host to a succession of visitors.

In the summer of 1940 troops of the Durham Light Infantry were billeted there. Residents soon became used to finding soldiers training in the most unexpected places, practising camouflage amongst the vegetables, engaged in unarmed combat and bayonet practice in the school playground or carefully choosing the right spot to take up the prone shooting position in the cow pasture below the Court.

After the British troops had left for active service, elements of the United States Army arrived in July 1942. These were mainly staff of the Signal Corps, who spent their day working in offices at Benhall. They had their meals and slept in the Nissen huts, though eventually some were also billeted in local private homes. Their orderly room and a dark-panelled day room were situated in the Court. For a brief time the Hollywood film actor Mickey Rooney was one of their number. He disappeared after a couple of days and it was assumed that he had been transferred to another location, where training films were being made.

In due course the Court came to be occupied by staff of the US Services of Supply. Their duties involved planning first for the invasion of North Africa and then for the Normandy landings. Most of them were transferred to Paris in September 1944.

One of the former GIs recalls that Leckhampton was his favourite camp by far, partly because of its superb location and the splendid manor house, but mainly because of the friendly and welcoming attitude of the local residents, who made the American soldiers feel very much at home. After the war was over, at least one of them married a local girl, and others have kept up their contacts with Leckhampton

Following the departure of the Americans, the Court remained unoccupied for a time. Although Italian prisoners of war are known to have been present in the area, working on local farms, they were not accommodated at Leckhampton Court but are believed to have been brought over from camps at Ullenwood or Swindon Village.

German Prisoners of War

The camp underwent a revival during the period between 1945 and 1948, when it was the Headquarters of 263 Working Camp for German prisoners of war, who were being held for screening and political re-education prior to repatriation. During this time they worked mostly on local farms or occasionally mended roads or felled timber.

The capacity of the camp itself was over 500, but more were billeted in local farms or hostels in the wider area. The Court itself was largely used by the British Army administrative staff. The great majority of prisoners were accommodated in Nissen huts in the grounds, to the left of the driveway leading up from the Lower Lodge. The camp kitchen stood in front of the entrance gates of the Court, and below it was the motor transport pool. Vehicles were repaired in the old coach house. The huts to the right of the driveway housed, amongst other things, tailor's and carpenter's workshops, a theatre, a medical centre, a chapel, washrooms and toilets, and the administration and camp leader's hut. There was a guard post just inside the entrance.

The prisoner of war camp was opened on 6 September 1945. A former inmate's diary shows that the first three months saw it transformed from an empty site to something of a showpiece.

A delightful pond, fountain and garden were built in a corner by St Peter's Church, where prisoners would congregate in their free time. The remains of the fountain are still visible, as are traces of the open-air skittle alley which was built in the same vicinity. In the recent past, the fountain has been renovated and a small area around it fenced off.

In due course, restrictions at the camp were eased and in April 1947 a recital of organ and church music was given by some prisoners in St Peter's Church. A party of volunteers refurbished the Parish Hall, distempering and painting it, rearranging the lighting and rebuilding the stage. At a social evening held there in June 1947, the Rector thanked the prisoners for their magnificent efforts. The camp band provided the music during the refreshments and dancing that followed.

By that time, the barbed-wire fence which surrounded the camp was more a means of keeping the cows out than restraining the inmates. Many, however, chose to stay on site and made various things such as furniture, lamps, toys, canvas slippers and models, from any materials that came to hand and which were purchased by local people. Others painted, sketched or enjoyed gardening, and many took part in plays or concerts given regularly at the Parish Hall, with the German camp spokesman usually acting as compère. There was also a camp football team which regularly played local sides on the primary school playing field.

Some of the prisoners were active Christians and took great pride in their camp chapel, which was simply furnished with benches and a wooden altar. The men also marched to normal services in St. Peter's, where they sat at the back of the church. The Parish Magazine records that on 22 September 1946, 250 prisoners held a harvest service there, their padre standing in the pulpit with a white ensign behind him.

The camp closed on 22 May 1948. Some former inmates were later to return permanently to England, among them five who married local girls. Others have also returned to revisit a place where, as young men barely out of their teens, they spent their formative years. By a curious twist, one of the British officers in charge of the Germans had himself arrived from Germany in 1939, at the age of 13, on one of the so-called *Kindertransports*.

Above, *the drawing room in about 1896. This photograph was taken by Miss de Lacy Lacy, a friend of Muriel Hargreaves and a frequent visitor to the Court.* Below, *the same room as a library, probably when set out for the sale in 1956*
(*Elwes Family Archive*)

5 Leckhampton Court School

The Court and the requisitioned land were in a poor condition after their service during the Second World War, and the cost of repair and restoration would have exceeded what the government was prepared to pay by way of compensation. After Mrs Elwes's death in 1955, the Court and 'Park' were offered for sale but there were no takers, not even at an auction held in March 1956. However, Dr Paul Saunders, who was looking for larger accommodation for the preparatory boarding school which he and his American-born wife were running in Cheltenham, took a lease on the building. The school remained there for the next dozen years, Dr Saunders having exercised the right to buy in 1962.

After some essential repairs had been carried out to the building, on 11 March 1957 the pupils moved there from Keynsham Priors in London Road and Leckhampton Court School was founded.

There were usually about five teachers and fifty pupils ranging in age between about 10 and 16. A few of these lived locally and were day

39

boys, but the great majority, at least in the early days of the school, were boarders. Many were recruited from overseas with a view to qualifying at Dartmouth or Sandhurst. After the erection of the Berlin Wall in 1961 the Saunders wrote to the German Embassy inviting twelve escapees from East Germany to the school, all of whom proved to be excellent and hard-working.

The boys were pressed hard academically and caned for not doing homework, in keeping with the headmaster's 'Victorian and classical tradition', as reported in the Gloucestershire Echo. The uniform consisted of a black, yellow and red-striped blazer with complementary tie and black mortar-board.

Of the staff, only Dr and Mrs Saunders lived at the school, in 'Fletcher's Cottage'. In the early years, the rooms upstairs in the 'Tudor Wing' were dormitories or individual bedrooms and small classrooms. The 'King's Wing' was divided into classrooms upstairs with a large and grand library downstairs, used for private study and examinations and for ceremonial occasions, such as speech days. Two further classrooms were situated near the kitchens. The small sitting room inside the main entrance was known as 'the Pink Room' and was used for interviews and entertaining visiting parents.

The old banqueting hall was used as the school dining room, for which Mrs Saunders did all the cooking. A large gong summoned the boys to table. The banqueting hall was also used for special occasions, when Dr and Mrs Saunders and any VIPs occupied seats in the minstrel gallery.

The now ruined coach house was at that time in good repair and was filled with Victorian furniture, which fascinated the boys. What is now 'Goose Bay' was used as a store for hay by the farmer who rented the nearby meadows. The geese, which were a feature of the Court even after the Saunders had left it, used to roam about freely both outside and occasionally even inside the building.

The school curriculum was fairly standard, with the teachers being responsible for more than one subject each. During the afternoons the pupils had free periods during which they helped maintain the Court and gardens and tended the assorted animals and geese. Neither Lower nor Middle Lodge was occupied and they were used as 'dens'. Tower Lodge was sold by the Elwes family trustees in 1961, followed by Lower Lodge in 1964.

One former pupil recalls that a major task was to clear the lake of débris dumped there during the war, a job which the boys relished because 'they always ended up covered from head to toe in mud'. There was a small boat which they were allowed to use and, during the hard winter of 1962-63, skating on the frozen lake proved a popular pastime.

There were limited sports facilities available: a table-tennis room and, beside the banqueting hall, where part of the Georgian mansion had once stood, a neglected tennis court which later on was used mostly for football. Drill-style physical training was performed in the main courtyard, the boys all immaculately dressed in white. A popular geography and games teacher, Captain Masterman, would sometimes jog with the boys to the top of Leckhampton Hill for a game of football before they completed the cross-country run back to the Court. Cricket was often played on a meadow near the Court, with the boys mowing the wicket themselves. Otherwise organised cricket and rugby took place on Burrow's Field, usually in Junior and Senior School groups.

The atmosphere of the building encouraged both boys and masters to sense ghostly presences. Dr Saunders too enjoyed telling of footsteps heard in the night, glimpses of a cavalier's turned-down boots and even of his wife's purse being moved overnight from under her pillow to the bathroom.

In 1967 Dr Saunders became very much involved with a campaign to save the historic heart of Cheltenham from would-be developers. In order to become a town councillor he had to take up residence in Cheltenham and leave Mrs Saunders on her own at the Court. He eventually found that his preoccupation with the campaign left too little time for running the school and in 1969 it closed its doors for good. (He was particularly concerned about St George's Place which he described as having once been 'a kind of Harley Street' and where for a time Dr Edward Jenner had had a surgery. He published an account in *Edward Jenner: the Cheltenham Years, 1795–1820*. Charles Brandon Trye would have been pleased to know that Jenner's name was again being celebrated at the Court.)

The Saunders continued to own the Court but it was difficult to secure such a large building, and over the next few years it had fallen into an alarming state of decay, helped considerably by the action of vandals. In due course it was engulfed by vegetation, and saplings grew from the eaves. There was damage by water from above and below, all forms of rot were rampant, and the floors were giving way. In 1976 the decision was taken to sell the Court to the Sue Ryder Foundation.

The Ruined Banqueting Hall in 1977

Goose Bay today

6   The Sue Ryder Care Centre

It was by a stroke of good fortune that Leckhampton Court was on the market just when Lady Ryder was looking for a suitable home to provide continuing care for patients of the Radiotherapy Centre at Cheltenham General Hospital. As a result, the Court was saved from the threat of demolition and the Foundation was able to go some way towards satisfying a desperate local need for after-care. The purchase was concluded in 1977, with the aid of a repair grant from the Historic Buildings Council, other supporting organisations and hundreds of voluntary subscribers.

In her autobiography *Child of My Love*, Sue Ryder included her own graphic account of the heroic efforts to clear and secure the site and to plan and execute the building's conversion. On one of her early visits, she learned from Mrs Saunders that the roof of the hall had collapsed.

The work teams camped

H R H Prince Charles and Lady Ryder (*Courtesy of* The Gloucestershire Echo)

in Fletcher's Cottage, the only section of the building that remained intact, and used a hut in the courtyard as an office. The main contractor was Thomas Williams Ltd, whose senior partner, Cecil Williams, later became Chairman of the Foundation's fundraising team for the area. The plans were drawn up by the Foundation's own team of architects, led by Mr Alan Wilson. Many years later one of his team, Richard Sale, had occasion to visit his uncle, who was a patient at the Court, and his tribute is reproduced on a later page.

The demanding problems faced by the architects and the solutions they devised were described in articles in the *Architects' Journal*. The brief was that the total cost was not to exceed that of purpose-building on a green field site. The work of restoration was to have as long a life as practicable, using materials and methods of construction that matched the original. The only major departure from this policy was the decision to use laminated pine frames, beams and rafters in the chapel – an elegant contemporary solution where it would have been uneconomical to reconstruct completely. It was also a requirement to create the atmosphere of a private home, discreetly supported by facilities for 'heavy nursing', while ensuring the highest degree of fire safety for immobile patients. Though the extent of damage and defect turned out to be far greater than superficial inspection could have suggested, the work was carried out with great skill and dedication, and the results were recognised in 1981 when the Court and annex received the top award in the country for the use of natural stone in conservation and restoration.

The ruined stable block, nicknamed 'Goose Bay' after its earlier occupants, was converted first, utilising as much as possible of the original stonework and timbers. It was opened to receive nine patients on St George's Day 1980. At an open day held the previous autumn one of the visitors was Mrs Judith Green of Chedworth, a daughter of Cecil and Muriel Elwes, who had been born at the Court. In October 1981 the Tudor (South) Wing was opened, followed in 1983 by the King's (North) Wing, bringing the total number of beds at that time to forty-two.

The first Matron was Mrs Dorothy Green, who had already spent seven years nursing cancer patients at the Cobalt Unit of Cheltenham General Hospital. The Honorary Medical Director was Dr Fred Hanna (in his capacity as head of the Cobalt Unit); he was followed in 1978 by Dr David Mahy. The direction of the Home was initially in the hands of a House Committee consisting largely of lay people. Cecil Williams, Dr David Mahy and Keith Newcombe served in succession as its Chairman. Mrs Avril Hastings was Administrator throughout the period 1982–2001.

A Group of Nurses and Helpers, 1984
(*Courtesy of* The Gloucestershire Echo)

In April 1983 the chapel was dedicated by the Bishop of Gloucester, and the Abbot of Prinknash and a representative of the Free Churches also participated. A member of the local clergy is attached to the Centre as chaplain and visits the patients regularly as well as holding prayer meetings, conducting services and giving holy communion. Other clergy are welcome to visit the patients and their families at any time. The chapel is also used for other functions, such as concerts, lectures and exhibitions, and it is always crammed with stalls and customers during fundraising events.

In 1988 it was decided to convert Goose Bay into a 'Day Care Centre', described at the time as providing 'companionship and a safe, pleasant and comfortable environment for patients in the community to spend the day'. All in-patient care has since been concentrated in the main building, providing at present eighteen beds. An alternative scheme, for a purpose-built day centre, had been rejected as too expensive and out of keeping with its setting.

Royal Visits and Prince Charles's Patronage

In 1984 the Home was honoured with a visit by the Princess of Wales and later by Prince and Princess Michael of Kent. In 1986 His Royal

Highness the Prince of Wales agreed to become Patron. His visits to the Court – usually around Christmas time – are always regarded as a red letter day by patients and their families, staff and other carers. Lady Ryder used also to be present on most of these occasions. In 1992 the Prince unveiled a plaque commemorating his visit to the new Day Care Unit. He congratulated all who had been involved in establishing and running the unit, commenting also that 'this country would grind to a halt without the many and generous efforts of volunteers'.

Re-branding as 'Sue Ryder Care'

In September 2000 the organisation's headquarters at Cavendish announced that the original name, The Sue Ryder Foundation, was felt to have become somewhat dated and did not appear to reflect accurately the charity's work nationwide. The general public, for example, was more aware of the Foundation's charity shops than of its care centres. It was felt on the other hand that all the characteristics

H R H the Princess of Wales, Prince and Princess Michael of Kent
(*Courtesy of* The Gloucestershire Echo)

that were dear to the organisation were encompassed in the word 'Care'. The Court came to be seen as a *hospice* from that time, providing care to those patients whose symptoms and needs are not being relieved in the home or any other care setting. The focus is on assessment of the patient by a range of professions, management of symptoms, rehabilitation and terminal care.

Fundraising

The Care Centre is not part of the National Health Service, though both the Cheltenham and Gloucester Health Authorities do make a small contribution to running costs. A considerable income is received from covenants, legacies and donations, but a substantial sum has still to be raised each year by the support groups and the Care Centre's own fundraising activities.

Local fundraising has been crucial to the financial viability of the Care Centre from the outset. During the first eighteen months after Sue Ryder launched her appeal in 1977, a committee led by Miss Peggy Challis raised £167,000. A Friends' Association was established and led to the formation of support groups of which there were at one time as many as twenty-one throughout Gloucestershire, Worcestershire and Herefordshire.

Apart from achieving their aim of raising funds, the events and activities have served to bring together members of the community. The Queen's Golden Jubilee party at the Court attracted people from all sections of Leckhampton and revived memories of the Summer Fêtes hosted by John Hargreaves. Some occasions have established themselves as regular entries in the calendar, notably the Open Day held in September, billed as a 'Medieval Fayre', with the more theatrical participants being dressed in suitable costume, and the Gloucestershire Morris Men and a jazz band enlivening the atmosphere. Other events, some under the slogan of 'Share the Care', include, in no particular order: Boxing Day fun runs, 'Ride for Ryder' cycle runs, street and house-to-house collections, raffles, auctions, fashion shows, art exhibitions (one of them including the auction of one of Prince Charles's paintings), concerts (which performers usually look forward to as much as the audiences), flower festivals, talks, sponsored marathons, coffee mornings, luncheons, supper evenings, balloon rides, parachute jumps, an air show, opera and theatrical performances at country houses, cards and calendars illustrating the Court and its surroundings ... and books written in aid of the cause(!).

During most of the Care Centre's existence, the driving force behind these activities has been the Appeals Co-ordinator Mrs Gillian Rose. She has been tireless in her encouragement and has usually been present and able to introduce the proceedings and thank the speaker or performer with a few well chosen words. Though she has recently retired from that position, she is continuing to serve in the rôle of Chairman of the Friends. A notable predecessor was the late James Graham, with for many years the late Jean Bendall as Honorary Secretary and Miss Margaret Witcomb as Honorary Treasurer.

The Embroidery

Over a period of five years a team of ladies worked on three embroidery panels showing a cross-section of life at the Sue Ryder Care Centre. The embroidery measures 8 feet high by 6 feet across and was designed by Ros Arno from an original idea by Mrs Mary Cooper and Mrs Gillian Rose. It was unveiled in the chapel in 1995.

The Gardens and Surroundings

Numerous helpers, including the Cotswold Wardens under John Millington (now the Chairman of the Advisory Committee) assisted by Allan Wood, not only maintain the neat appearance of the surroundings but have extended the flower borders, cleared the lake of weeds and established a plantation of trees. A fuller account of their work is provided in the following chapter.

The Sue Ryder Care Centre Today

Patients can be admitted on the recommendation of their doctor, hospital consultant or district nurse. This may be for periods of convalescence both during and after treatment or for short-term respite care to allow relatives to take a rest or holiday. In-patients are accommodated either in bays or single rooms and, as well as receiving nursing and medical care, are attended by a physiotherapist, complementary therapists and a social worker. A liaison nurse is responsible for contact with a patient's doctor and family. There are facilities for the special care needed by those with cancer in its final stages. At the Day Hospice, staff and volunteers offer the opportunity of companionship, creative and therapeutic activities. The aim is to achieve an atmosphere of love, compassion, unhurried care and understanding of each individual patient's needs.

The Embroidery (detail)
(Michael Charity)

THE FUTURE

by Jo Blackburn, the Care Centre Manager

The Sue Ryder Care Centre at Leckhampton Court is a voluntary and non-profit making organisation, whose future is dependent on the support of local fundraisers and 'purchasers'. With the changes that have recently taken place in the National Health Service our purchasers have become predominantly the Primary Healthcare Trusts. As purchasers, they require us to provide a service that is responsive to and reflects the needs of the local community.

Current Government policy has also created a national debate as to the definition of supportive and palliative care for people with cancer. The NHS Cancer Plan (2000) in the chapter on Improving Care refers only to a Supportive Care Strategy, whilst later policy documents do recognise the unique and distinct contribution to cancer care of hospice and specialist palliative care services. This differentiation is crucial to the debate as to how Leckhampton Court will develop in the future. Our current position as a health care provider will be influenced by the implementation and interpretation of the Cancer Plan at a local level and the purchaser's desire to support the 'right' type of care for those people in Gloucestershire who have cancer or a life-threatening illness. Whilst one cannot doubt the future of Leckhampton Court as the hospice for Gloucestershire, the term hospice may come to reflect a philosophy of care rather than a building or a service.

Our vision of becoming the Specialist Palliative Care Unit for Gloucestershire will demand a significant commitment both from Sue Ryder Care as an organisation and financially from our purchasers. A Specialist Palliative Care Unit would require a full multi-professional specialist team, comprising a consultant, senior nursing staff, social worker, physiotherapist, occupational therapist, psychologist and chaplain, all with experience and qualifications in palliative care. In addition we would need to address the shortcomings in our current building, particularly those failing to meet the requirements of the Care Standards Act (2000). Despite the fact that our future is fraught with bureaucratic and political issues we are fortunate to have a voice at the appropriate tables, whether locally or nationally. The high standard of care that we provide at Leckhampton Court will continue whilst we will strive to make our vision a reality for the people of Gloucestershire.

7 The Grounds Today

John Millington, Chairman of the Advisory Committee supporting the Sue Ryder Care Centre, has provided the following account.

Landscaped and planted grounds form a delightful backdrop to the Court with its mellow honey-coloured stonework. The Kip engraving shows that the patterns of three hundred years ago have not been completely obscured. Of course, at that time farming shaped the landscape, with the pleasure garden largely on the east side of the main building.

Today the grounds divide into two parts: the gardens that surround the buildings, and the wilder area near the lake, known as Dogkennel Wood. These planted areas contribute enormously to the ambience but also supply an outdoor recreational area with benches for patients, staff and visitors. The lawns and terraces are invaluable for outdoor fundraising events.

The few employed staff are supplemented by three regular teams of volunteer helpers: the gardeners who look after the borders and planted beds, the Ground Force Team who carry out heavier work such as wall building and path construction, and the Cotswold Voluntary Wardens who care for the Dogkennel Wood land. Other groups, notably the employees of Zurich Insurance, have also provided help.

The gardens near the buildings, including the drives and parking areas, occupy about five acres. Interest and colour are provided by the shrub borders, and by the rose beds and spring bulbs. Trees in these areas include limes, yew, sycamore, walnut, beech, hornbeam, ash, pine and chestnut. Many are protected specimens, and some of them are particularly elegant examples.

Recently, the ground to the south of the Court, once an orchard and vegetable garden, has been grassed over and is being planted as a new arboretum. Old walls form two sheltered courtyards adjacent to the Tudor wing where more delicate plants can be nurtured.

The lake with its brick dam and weir seems to have been built in the Victorian period, and the Kip engraving indicates that there were formerly several interconnected ponds, perhaps leading to an estate mill. The lake is fed by streams flowing all year round. Excavation for the present garage and the Day Hospice conservatory has shown that there have been many changes in this 'home farm' area and that the ground has been significantly raised.

Beyond the lake is Dogkennel Wood. This area of about nine acres is mainly woodland, with a meadow in view of the Day Care Centre. The lower section, on the lower lias clays, is very wet. Paths have been cleared so that visitors can enjoy the view from this quiet wildlife sanctuary. The meadow is fenced and maintained by grazing with sheep in the growing season, and this also provides interest for patients.

Within the wood there are remains of a ditch and bank boundary, traces of old tracks, and some indications that clay has been dug out

'Fletcher's Cottage' today

A team of volunteers repairing a wall

from the upper area for pond construction. Lines of trees indicate old hedges within which hazels were planted to provide a supply of coppice wood for the estate. A dozen varieties of tree are established in the wood, and ninety-nine species of plant and fifteen varieties of grass have been identified. As this area is frequented by deer, and there are badger setts towards the south west corner, the main aim of preservation work has been to retain a diversity of wildlife.

After careful and extensive clearing work it was decided in 1993 to double the size of the wooded area. The public generously gave the money to pay for the trees, rabbit guards and stakes, and many came to the site to plant their own tree. In all some 650 trees were installed comprising oak, beech, alder, black poplar, small leaved lime, birch and ash: all native species. This was a highly successful event and over 95 per cent of the trees have survived and flourished.

The grounds of Leckhampton Court provide an amenity which is valued by the local community almost as much as the old manor house itself. They are together an asset to the landscape and a piece of history that can be seen and touched, but much more than that, they constitute an invaluable facility which gives care to the sick in a very special way.

At a Medieval Fayre: Morris
Dancers and a bookstall

8 Personal Impressions of the Court

From William Felton Norwood, a pediatrician living in Atlanta, Georgia, USA, and a descendant of William Norwood 'the Emigrant':

Leckhampton Court – just the name itself conjures up all sorts of fanciful, imaginative, and romantic notions in the mind of most any American and especially in one with English forebears. As a twelfth-generation direct descendant of William Norwood, I was enchanted and delighted on first seeing the manor. It was just as I had supposed it might be ... it seemed so much in keeping with the spirit and character of our family.

I felt at ease and in harmony with Leckhampton Court and the stability it seemed to impart. Who is to say that there is not more passed to us via DNA than we might possibly imagine?

It gives me great pleasure as a physician to know that the manor is being used to provide care and service to those in need, and I commend everyone associated with Leckhampton Court in this new rôle it is playing.

From the Reverend Matthew Thomas Locy Corkern, an Episcopal priest living in McLean, Virginia, USA, another descendant of William Norwood:

Through visits and in imagination, Leckhampton Court has long been to me a place of heritage – perhaps, of ancestral homage. Indeed, even after seven centuries, this astonishing architectural amalgam serves as a living testimony to the political, spiritual, economic, and cultural influences that have dominated daily life in Gloucestershire. With such a legacy to admire, my paternal grandfather recounted tales of this magical place and our Norwood ancestry.

Pride of place and family cause you to seek some sense of the occupants who once lived, loved, fought, prayed and died here. You walk the old garden paths and take snapshots of architectural eccentricities left from ages gone. Then you follow the avenue that leads down to St Peter's Church, where you may glimpse – and perhaps be overwhelmed by – the ancient patrician attitudes exemplified by the intricately wrought brass and memorial tombs of the prosperous, pious, and prolific 'lords of the manor'.

This historic country house has evolved into a truly sacred site of refuge for those who come to visit and for those who come to stay. Moving from its past, this welcoming house continues to evoke the twin pillars of serenity and hospitality. As a priest who preaches that 'we are all heirs through hope of God's eternal kingdom', I am moved and amazed at how God is glorified in the 'new' Leckhampton Court, and at how each person is received on crossing the threshold.

From Dr David Maby, formerly Consultant in Radiotherapy and Oncology at Cheltenham General Hospital and Honorary Medical Director at Leckhampton Court:

Dr David Maby

In 1978 I had lived in Leckhampton for over ten years and worked as a cancer specialist in Cheltenham. I knew virtually nothing about Leckhampton Court but that it was partly in ruins and tales of haunting were used to discourage children from trespassing there. It was about then that I received a knock on the door and the Chairman of the Parish Council (James Graham) told me there was to be a public meeting at Leckhampton Primary School to hear Sue Ryder speak. She was to tell of her plans to use the Court as a home for cancer patients, too ill to go home but not in need of active treatment. I met her at the door of the meeting – and was asked to speak first! Since then I have maintained an interest in the Court. It became of great help to us at the Gloucestershire Cancer Centre from 1980 onwards, when we were very short of beds and the nearest facility providing palliative cancer care was in South Wales. As the policy and support for home care of many cancer patients has developed, fewer beds are now in use at Leckhampton but the homely environment and the specialist care offered there still provide an essential service to many in-patients and day care cancer patients in Gloucestershire.

From Mrs Gillian Rose, who for over 20 years was Appeals Co-ordinator:

Gillian Rose

My first view of Leckhampton Court was on a Spring day in 1982. I saw a beautiful, ancient stone and timber building, with an air of serenity, which was echoed when I went inside. That feeling of tranquillity is often commented upon and I certainly felt it immediately.

I knew of Sue Ryder's work and of her idealistic attitude to the provision of professional, loving care for all patients, whatever their creed or colour, in beautiful, homely surroundings. I was glad to support this place and those values through fundraising and public relations and – like several others – to make it more than a job, more a part of my life.

From the beginning there was a dedicated group of staff and volunteers who supported the completion of the Home and its development as Gloucestershire's only hospice able to provide in-patient care. Matron Green, Avril Hastings, Peggy Challis, Dr David Mahy, James Graham and Ken Tomlinson, Jean Bendall, Allan Wood, Margaret Witcomb and Cecil Williams were outstanding people who really cared about what was offered to patients from our community; they also wished to support the excellent staff in the delivery of that care. All were inspired by and in some cases personally 'gathered in' by Lady Ryder to help in the project she called 'Pilgrim's Progress'.

Fundraising was not easy, even for such a worthwhile cause, but early on I was thrilled to make the successful bid for the major prize of £10,000 in the Severn Sound Money Mountain. That allowed the completion of the chapel and of King's Wing, which was furnished by a local Round Table and the Painswick Support Group.

There were special events in the chapel, which must be an ideal setting for a small group of musicians or a soloist. Mary O'Hara and Jane Lapotaire both performed there and Gyles Brandreth entertained, a local group presented a tribute to Noel Coward, another an Olde Time Music Hall. It was particularly pleasing if an event could allow the participation and enjoyment of patients. After a display and sale by the Cotswold Orchid Society, stems of orchids were cut to give each patient a special flower at the bedside.

The patronage of the Prince of Wales has been a particular honour for Leckhampton Court. Imagine my pleasure when my simple letter to His Royal Highness, requesting his patronage for our Home, received a prompt and positive reply. The Prince's annual visits over many years have helped to boost the morale of patients and their families and the staff.

I had an ambition to organise volunteers to execute an embroidery for Leckhampton Court. As I am not, myself, an embroiderer, my explanations and illustrations to an invited group left a lot to be desired. Luckily Mary Cooper was among the group and she introduced embroidery designer Ros Arno. Mary and Ros worked on the design and broke it down into components which several embroiderers worked on before the whole was assembled on to the background. We were able to obtain a free workshop at Sudeley Castle on the understanding that it would be manned and open to the public at regular hours. Mary and I and several others worked on background embroidery at Sudeley for a year and sold stitches to hundreds of the public, who also signed the back of the canvas; thus we funded the work, which has been giving interest and pleasure for many years.

My memoir is, of necessity, a miscellany of impressions about this Home which has given a great deal of excellent service to this community and of the people who have made it possible so far. Perhaps each of those who worked so hard may take a little of the credit for that, together with Lady Ryder, who had the foresight, drive and compassion to set this beautiful old house on its current course.

From Digby Dones, who was moved to write as a patient's relative, whose experience has inspired him to become a committed member of the Friends of Leckhampton Court:

Just over a year ago, my brother Peter died at Leckhampton Court, aged 39. He was lucky! He was lucky to have been there and even more lucky that at the end a wonderful nurse held his hand and stroked his cheek and told him not to worry. My sister, father and I were lucky too. For in the days and weeks after Peter's death there was always someone at Leckhampton Court to hold our hands and talk to us and let us grieve.

I decided I wanted to do something to help, so I joined the Friends of Leckhampton Court. The Friends support the work of the Care Centre by raising funds to purchase items which will help the comfort and care of the patients and ease the work of the nursing staff. For many years the Friends have paid for the maintenance and running of a wheelchair bus and this year we have bought a special chair at a cost of approximately £1,000.

Leckhampton Court particularly needs the support of all of us whose lives have been touched by it, so please join the Friends in memory of your loved one, so that others may benefit from its work.

From Mr Harry Grenville, who was a member of the British permanent staff at the prisoner of war camp in 1948:

I have very happy memories of Leckhampton Court with its potpourri of architectural styles. My room was under a twisted red-brick Tudor chimney and looked over towards the Malvern Hills. I used to enjoy playing records of Elgar on summer evenings while looking across to his countryside. Climbing up to the top of Leckhampton Hill and walking along the edge of the escarpment was another of my favourite pursuits, as it was for the Germans who were not subjected to many restrictions at that late stage. Unless I mis-remember this, members of the Elwes family occasionally turned up, probably to make sure we were looking after the place properly. I am sure we did.'

From Karl Wolf, who was the official spokesman for the German prisoners of war, 1945–1948 (and who with his German wife later came to live and work in Cheltenham):

My experience at the camp left a lasting impression. The Commandant, Major Harris, was a very fair and just gentleman, and the prisoners enjoyed a period of wellbeing and contentment under his command in unfortunate circumstances. He belonged to a generation of gentlemen who made this country great. He was instrumental in promoting the arts and was very interested in history at a time when free speech was an unknown phenomenon to Germans of my generation. It is fair to say that contact with him and his fellow officers brought back a sense of personal dignity to all of us.

From Richard Sale, who as a young architect worked on the reconstruction of the Court:

Snow was falling and the wind was icy, but my colleague and I decided we would drive from Cavendish for our first visit to Leckhampton Court. It was 1978 and I was part of a small team of architects working within The Sue Ryder Foundation. Our job was to convert both the stable block and the main building to provide accommodation for cancer patients.

By the time we finished our journey, the snow had settled and was several inches deep. As we drove up the hill to Leckhampton Court, I was struck by what appeared to be little more than a romantic ruin. The snow covered everything and in the low light it was difficult to make out what was building and what wasn't. Only a small part [Fletcher's Cottage] had a roof, and this is where we were meant to spend the night. In a damp room under the roof several beds, with piles of eiderdowns, were provided for us. Remember this was The Sue Ryder Foundation, everything was donated, and personal sacrifice was an unspoken aspect of the job description. But I like some comfort, especially at night, so we left Leckhampton and slept on the floor of my grandmother's flat in Cheltenham. We got up early the next morning and returned to the ruin. In the full daylight it was a little easier to make out the state of the building.

Now I love clambering over building sites, making sense in my mind of what is and what could be. I also love ancient domestic buildings. So this was a real treat. A huge oak roof truss lay collapsed on an upper floor, late medieval perhaps, covered in snow. The great chapel window was close to collapse too. Ivy covered much of the building. I have a vague memory of a beautiful Georgian staircase. Numerous windows of different styles and periods provided clues about the age of the different wings of the building. Gradually I built up a picture of how the Court had been extended and adapted over the years. We were simply the next characters in the story, the twentieth-century designers. How could we respect our predecessors' work and bring the building up to modern standards?

We spent time drawing the chapel window, recording every individual stone, so that it could be taken down and rebuilt. We discussed the shape of special bricks that were made to rebuild the Tudor chimneystacks. I think they were donated to the charity by the brick makers. We wondered about lifts and ramps to allow wheelchairs through the building. Back at the office I designed staircases and cupboards, helped plan the landscaping of the courtyard – and soon moved on to other jobs. Leckhampton started to fade from my memory.

Nearly twenty years later I visited my uncle, also an architect, as he spent the last few months of his life at Leckhampton, cared for by staff, volunteers and family. I remember sitting with him in an upstairs sitting room. Above us was the medieval roof truss that had collapsed and been covered with snow – now fully restored and back in its rightful place.

Competitors set off on in the annual 'Fun Run' (*Courtesy of* The Gloucestershire Echo)

Bibliography

Eve Andrew and Eric Brewin, *Leckhampton through the Ages*, 1984

Robert Cary Barnard, *Records of Leckhampton*, 1897

Laura Beatty, *Lillie Langtry*, 1999

David Bick, *Old Leckhampton* 1993

G Marion Norwood Callam, *The Norwoods, Vols I–III*, 1963–1997.

F Harrison, *Henry Norwood* (in *The Virginia Magazine*, January 1925)

Sydney Harrison (Ed), *Souvenir of Leckhampton Court V A Hospital*, 1919

Gwen Hart, *History of Cheltenham*, 1965

Nicholas Kingsley, *The Country Houses of Gloucestershire*, Volume 2, 1992

Lillie Langtry, *The Days I Knew*, Postscript by Chris Lake, 1989.

Daniel Lysons, *Sketch of the Life and Character of the late Charles Brandon Trye*, 1812

Alfred Miles, *History of Cheltenham*, Vol 5 p 88, Cheltenham Public Library

Eric Miller, *The History of Leckhampton Church*, 1989; *Leckhampton Yesteryear*, 1996; (Ed,
    with John Randall and Amy Woolacott), *Leckhampton in the Second World War*, 1998;
    (with Alan Gill) *Leckhampton in Old Photographs*, 2000

Terry Moore-Scott, unpublished article, *The Manorial Estates of Leckhampton*

Norden's Survey of the manor of Cheltenham, 1617

Henry Norwood, *A Voyage to Virginia*, from Churchill's *Voyages*, 1732

Maureen Norwood, *Francis Norwood, Immigrant to Massachusetts*, 1987

George Plumptre, *Edward VII*, 1995

Sue Ryder, *Child of my Love*, 1986

Paul Saunders, *Edward Jenner: the Cheltenham Years, 1795–1820*, 1982

Peter Southerton, *Hunting the Cotswold Stag*, Cheltenham LHS *Journal* No 14

Bruce Stait (Ed.), *Leckhampton 1894 – the End of an Era*, 1994

David Verey, *The Buildings of England, Gloucestershire: the Vale and the Forest of Dean*, 1980

Alan Wilson, Martin Meade, articles in the *Architects' Journal*, 17 March 1982

Amy Woolacott, *Foxhunting and the Leckhampton Court Foxhounds*, Leckhampton
    LHS Bulletin No 2, 2001

W H Wyndham Quin, *The Yeoman Cavalry of Gloucestershire and Monmouth*, 1898

Selected issues of *The Gloucestershire Echo, The Cheltenham Chronicle, The Cheltenham
Looker-on*

Most of the above are to be found in The Local Studies section of Cheltenham Reference
Library and/or The Gloucestershire Collection at Gloucester City Library.

Primary sources held in the Gloucestershire Record Office are included under the general
headings of D8831 (deposited by David Bick), D1388/SL3 & SL11, D1809, D2818,
D2970/91, D303 E&F, D5130/5/3, SL315.

Day Hospice Staff

From left to right. Top row: Jackie Reid, Nursing Auxiliary, *Robin Hosler,* Massage Therapist, *Maureen Canavan,* Nursing Auxiliary; *Middle row: Heather Burford,* Staff Nurse, *Gwyn Sloan,* Day Hospice Manager, *Irene Shoubridge,* Staff Nurse; *Bottom row: Rita Cook,* Nursing Auxiliary, *Alan Nicholson,* Transport Co-ordinator, *Louise Smail,* Reflexology Therapist.

Leckhampton Local History Society

Leckhampton Local History Society was founded in 1992. Its aims are to collect, study and publish information concerning the history of Leckhampton and to stimulate public interest in local history. It organises talks and discussions as well as outings and field trips, and there are opportunities to participate in research groups. It has produced several books and two substantial collections of research papers, complementing its quarterly newsletter, *Smoke Signal*.

Further information about the Society's activities may be obtained from the acting Honorary Secretary, Amy Woolacott, on Cheltenham 522566.

*　*　*

Eric Miller

Eric Miller is a founder member and past Chairman of the Society and is now its Co-ordinator of Research. Since his retirement from the Civil Service he has spent much of his time researching the history of Cheltenham and its environs. He has written books on the history of Leckhampton Church, on village life and events in Leckhampton and on Leckhampton in the Second World War (together with other members of the Society). In 2000, together with Alan Gill, he compiled *Britain in Old Photographs – Leckhampton*, which gained them an award from the Cheltenham Arts Council. He has also had articles on local history printed in a number of periodicals, including the journal of the British Association for Local History.